DUKE ELLINGTON STANDARDS

Piano Play-Along — Hal Leonard

PIANO | VOCAL | GUITAR • CD — VOLUME 38

CONTENTS

PAGE	TITLE	DEMO TRACK	PLAY-ALONG TRACK
2	Caravan	1	9
7	Do Nothin' Till You Hear from Me	2	10
10	I Got It Bad and That Ain't Good	3	11
15	In a Sentimental Mood	4	12
18	It Don't Mean a Thing (If It Ain't Got That Swing)	5	13
22	Love You Madly	6	14
28	Mood Indigo	7	15
25	Sophisticated Lady	8	16

Photo by William "PoPsie" Randolph
copyright 2006 Michael Randolph
www.PoPsiePhotos.com

ISBN-13: 978-0-634-08010-4
ISBN-10: 0-634-08010-5

HAL•LEONARD® CORPORATION
7777 W. BLUEMOUND RD. P.O. BOX 13819 MILWAUKEE, WI 53213

For all works contained herein:
Unauthorized copying, arranging, adapting, recording or public performance is an infringement of copyright.
Infringers are liable under the law.

Visit Hal Leonard Online at
www.halleonard.com

CARAVAN
from SOPHISTICATED LADIES

Words and Music by DUKE ELLINGTON,
IRVING MILLS and JUAN TIZOL

Moderately

Night_____ and stars a-bove that shine so bright_____ the mys-t'ry of their fad-ing light_____ that shines up-

Copyright © 1937 (Renewed 1965) and Assigned to Famous Music LLC and EMI Mills Music Inc. in the U.S.A.
Rights for the world outside the U.S.A. Controlled by EMI Mills Music Inc. (Publishing) and Warner Bros. Publications U.S. Inc. (Print)
International Copyright Secured   All Rights Reserved

on our car - a - van.

Sleep _____ up - on my shoul - der as we creep _____ a - cross the sands so I may keep _____

this mem-'ry of our car-a-van.

This is so ex-cit-ing you are so in-vit-ing

ing rest - ing in my arms as I thrill to the mag - ic charms of you, Be - side me *here beneath the blue my dream of love is coming true within our desert caravan.*

DO NOTHIN' TILL YOU HEAR FROM ME

Words and Music by DUKE ELLINGTON
and BOB RUSSELL

me. At least con-sid-er our ro-mance.

If you should take the word of oth-ers you've heard, I have-n't a chance.

True, I've been seen with some-one new, but does that mean that I'm un-true? When we're a-part, the words in my heart reveal how I feel about you.

Some kiss may cloud my memory, and other arms may hold a thrill.

But please do nothin' till you hear it from me, and you never will.

1. Do nothin' till you hear from
2.

I GOT IT BAD AND THAT AIN'T GOOD

Words by PAUL FRANCIS WEBSTER
Music by DUKE ELLINGTON

Am7 D13 4fr Am7 D7 F7 E7 Am7 D7
3
I have sought and my what a climb it is! My
3
Dm7 G7 G7♯5 Cmaj7 Am
3
life is just like the weath - er. It chang - es with the hours.
3
B7 Dm7 E7 A7 E♭7 D7
3
When he's near I'm fair and warm - er. When he's gone I'm cloud - y with show - ers.
3
G C7 G C7 G C7 G C7
In e - mo - tion, like the o - cean, it's ei - ther sink or swim, when a

wom - an loves a man like I love him. Never treats me
Like a lonely

sweet and gen - tle the way he should.
weep - ing wil - low, lost in the wood,

I got it bad and that ain't good!
I got it bad and that ain't good!

My poor heart is sen - ti - men - tal,
And the things I tell my pil - low,

not made of wood.   I got it
no wom-an should.   I got it

bad and that ain't good! _____ But
bad and that ain't good! _____ Though

when the week-end's o - ver and Mon - day rolls a -
folks with good in - ten - tions tell me to save my

roun', I end up like I start out, just
tears, I'm glad I'm mad a - bout him. I

14

cry - in' my heart out. He don't love me
can't live with - out him. Lord a - bove me,

like I love him, no - bod - y could.
make him love me, the way he should.

I got it bad and that ain't good.
I got it bad and that ain't

good.

IN A SENTIMENTAL MOOD

Words and Music by DUKE ELLINGTON,
IRVING MILLS and MANNY KURTZ

Dm Dm(maj7) Dm7 Dm6 Gm Gm(maj7)
3fr 3fr
kiss drifts a mel - o - dy so strange and sweet.
Gm7 C9 Dm D9 C♯dim/D Ddim D7
4fr 3fr
In this sen - ti - men - tal bliss you make my par - a -
Gm7 G♭7♭5 G♭7 F6 A♭13 D♭maj7 B♭m7
4fr
dise com - plete. Rose pet - als seem to fall, it's
E♭m7 G♭/A♭ A♭13 D♭ B♭9♯5 B♭13 E♭7♯5 E♭13 A♭7♯5 A♭13
6fr 4fr 6fr 5fr 4fr 4fr
all like a dream to call you mine.
3 3 3

17

IT DON'T MEAN A THING
(If It Ain't Got That Swing)

Words and Music by DUKE ELLINGTON
and IRVING MILLS

Lively

What good is mel-o-dy, what good is mu-sic, if it ain't pos-ses-sin' some-thing

Copyright © 1932 (Renewed 1959) and Assigned to Famous Music LLC and EMI Mills Music Inc. in the U.S.A.
Rights for the world outside the U.S.A. Controlled by EMI Mills Music Inc. (Publishing) and Warner Bros. Publications U.S. Inc. (Print)
International Copyright Secured   All Rights Reserved

sweet? It ain't the mel-o-dy, it ain't the mu-sic, there's some-thing else that makes the tune com-plete. It don't mean a thing if it ain't got that swing, (doo wah, doo wah, doo wah, doo wah, doo wah, _____ doo wah, doo wah, doo wah.) It don't mean a thing, _____ all you got to do is sing, (doo wah, ___ doo wah, doo wah, doo wah, doo wah, _____ doo wah, doo wah, doo wah.) It makes no diff'rence if _____ it's sweet or hot, _____

just give that rhy-thm ev-'ry-thing you got.

Oh, it don't mean a thing if it ain't got that swing, ___

(doo wah, ___ doo wah, doo wah, doo wah, doo wah, ___

___ doo wah, doo wah, doo wah.) It wah.)

LOVE YOU MADLY

By DUKE ELLINGTON

Medium bright Jump tempo

Love you madly, right or wrong. Sounds like the lyric of a song, but since it's so I thought you ought to know, I love you, love you madly. Better fish are

Copyright © 1950 (Renewed 1977) and Assigned to Famous Music LLC in the U.S.A.
Rights for the world outside the U.S.A. Controlled by Tempo Music, Inc. c/o Music Sales Corporation and Famous Music LLC
International Copyright Secured   All Rights Reserved

in the sea ___ is ___ not the the-o-ry ___ for me ___ and that's for sure. __ Just like I said be-fore, __ "I love you, love __ you mad- -ly." If you could see the hap-py you and me ___ I dream a-bout so proud - ly, __ you'd know the breath of spring __ that

24

SOPHISTICATED LADY
from SOPHISTICATED LADIES

Words and Music by DUKE ELLINGTON,
IRVING MILLS and MITCHELL PARISH

Copyright © 1933 (Renewed 1960) and Assigned to Famous Music LLC and EMI Mills Music Inc. in the U.S.A.
Rights for the world outside the U.S.A. Controlled by EMI Mills Music Inc. (Publishing) and Warner Bros. Publications U.S. Inc. (Print)
International Copyright Secured   All Rights Reserved

B♭m7
G♭7
F7
E7
E♭7
A♭maj7
Then, with dis - il - lu - sion deep in your eyes, you learned that
A♭7
4fr
G7
G♭7
F7
B♭7
E♭7
fools in love soon grow wise. The years have changed you, some - how; I
3
A♭
4fr
Am7♭5
D7
G
Em
see you now... Smok - ing, drink - ing, nev -
Am
D7
G
G♯dim7
Am7
D7♯5
- er think - ing of to - mor - row, non - cha - lant.

Dia-monds shin-ing, danc-ing, din-ing with some man in a res-tau-rant; is that all you real-ly want? No, So-phis-ti-cat-ed la-dy, I know, you miss the love you lost long a-go, and when no-bod-y is nigh you cry. They cry.

MOOD INDIGO
from SOPHISTICATED LADIES

Words and Music by DUKE ELLINGTON,
IRVING MILLS and ALBANY BIGARD

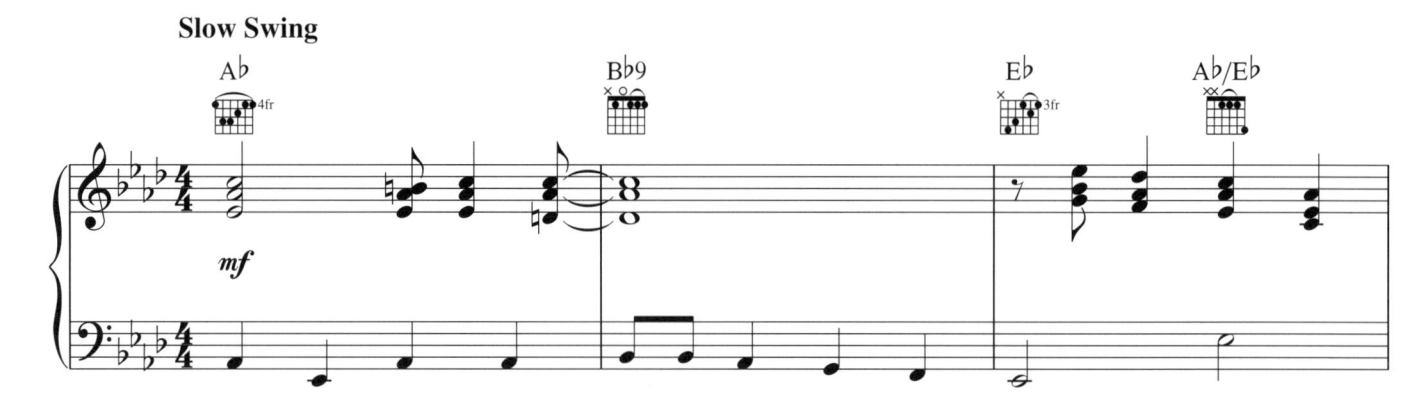

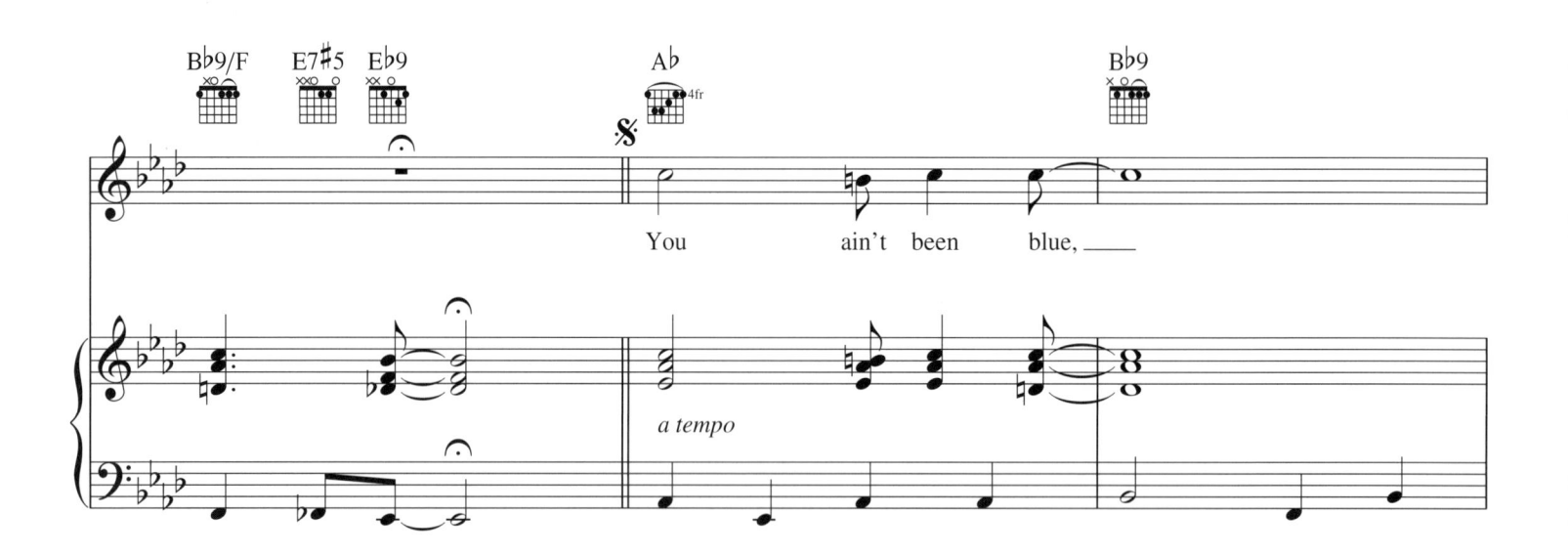

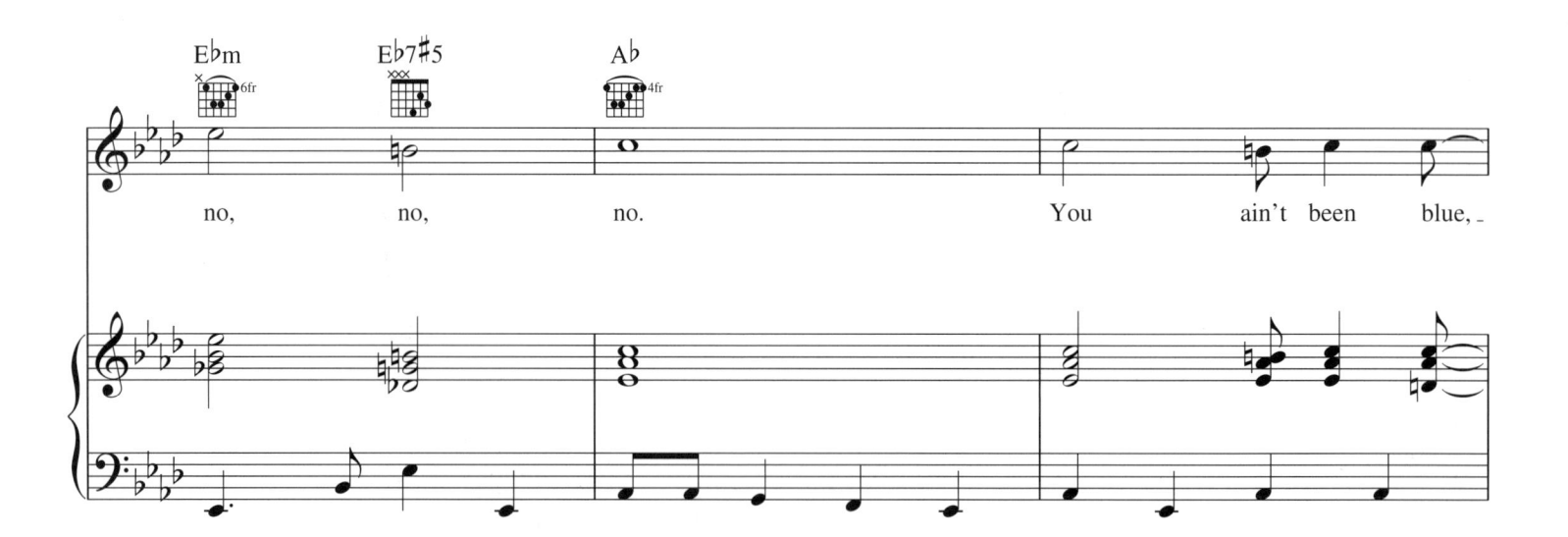

Slow Swing

You ain't been blue, no, no, no. You ain't been blue,

Copyright © 1931 (Renewed 1958) and Assigned to Famous Music LLC, EMI Mills Music Inc. and Indigo Mood Music c/o The Songwriters Guild Of America in the U.S.A.
Rights for the world outside the U.S.A. Controlled by EMI Mills Music Inc. (Publishing) and Warner Bros. Publications U.S. Inc. (Print)
International Copyright Secured All Rights Reserved

'til you've had that mood in-di-go. That feel-ing goes steal-in' down to my shoes, while I sit and sigh: "Go 'long, blues."

A♭ A♭dim7 A♭ B♭7
Al - ways get that mood in - di - go,
E♭9 D♭/E♭ E♭7 A♭/C Bdim7 B♭m7 E♭7 A♭ A♭dim7 A♭
since my ba - by said good - bye. In the eve - nin'
B♭7 B♭9/F E7♯5 E7 E♭7 D♭/F D♭m/F♭ E♭7
when lights are low, I'm so lone-some I could cry.
A♭7
'Cause there's no - bod - y who cares a - bout me,

I'm just a soul who's blu-er than blue can be. When I get that mood in-di-go, I could lay me down and die.

die.

"Go 'long blues."

THE ULTIMATE SONGBOOKS

HAL•LEONARD PIANO PLAY-ALONG

These great songbook/CD packs come with our standard arrangements for piano and voice with guitar chord frames plus a CD. The CD includes a full performance of each song, as well as a second track without the piano part so you can play "lead" with the band!

Vol. 1 Movie Music
Come What May • Forrest Gump – Main Title (Feather Theme) • My Heart Will Go On (Love Theme from Titanic) • The Rainbow Connection • Tears in Heaven • A Time for Us • Up Where We Belong • Where Do I Begin (Love Theme).
00311072 P/V/G $12.95

Vol. 2 Jazz Ballads
Autumn in New York • Do You Know What It Means to Miss New Orleans • Georgia on My Mind • In a Sentimental Mood • More Than You Know • The Nearness of You • The Very Thought of You • When Sunny Gets Blue.
00311073 P/V/G $12.95

Vol. 3 Timeless Pop
Ebony and Ivory • Every Breath You Take • From a Distance • I Write the Songs • In My Room • Let It Be • Oh, Pretty Woman • We've Only Just Begun.
00311074 P/V/G $12.95

Vol. 4 Broadway Classics
Ain't Misbehavin' • Cabaret • If I Were a Bell • Memory • Oklahoma • Some Enchanted Evening • The Sound of Music • You'll Never Walk Alone.
00311075 P/V/G $12.95

Vol. 5 Disney
Beauty and the Beast • Can You Feel the Love Tonight • Colors of the Wind • Go the Distance • Look Through My Eyes • A Whole New World • You'll Be in My Heart • You've Got a Friend in Me.
00311076 P/V/G $12.95

Vol. 6 Country Standards
Blue Eyes Crying in the Rain • Crazy • King of the Road • Oh, Lonesome Me • Ring of Fire • Tennessee Waltz • You Are My Sunshine • Your Cheatin' Heart.
00311077 P/V/G $12.95

Vol. 7 Love Songs
Can't Help Falling in Love • (They Long to Be) Close to You • Here, There and Everywhere • How Deep Is Your Love • I Honestly Love You • Maybe I'm Amazed • Wonderful Tonight • You Are So Beautiful.
00311078 P/V/G $12.95

Vol. 8 Classical Themes
Can Can • Habanera • Humoresque • In the Hall of the Mountain King • Minuet in G Major • Piano Concerto No. 21 in C Major, 2nd Movement Excerpt • Prelude in E Minor, Op. 28, No. 4 • Symphony No. 5 in C Minor, 1st Movement Excerpt.
00311079 Piano Solo $12.95

Vol. 9 Children's Songs
Do-Re-Mi • It's a Small World • Linus and Lucy • Sesame Street Theme • Sing • Winnie the Pooh • Won't You Be My Neighbor? • Yellow Submarine.
0311080 P/V/G $12.95

Vol. 10 Wedding Classics
Air on the G String • Ave Maria • Bridal Chorus • Canon in D • Jesu, Joy of Man's Desiring • Ode to Joy • Trumpet Voluntary • Wedding March.
00311081 Piano Solo $12.95

Vol. 11 Wedding Favorites
All I Ask of You • Don't Know Much • Endless Love • Grow Old with Me • In My Life • Longer • Wedding Processional • You and I.
00311097 P/V/G $12.95

Vol. 12 Christmas Favorites
Blue Christmas • The Christmas Song • Do You Hear What I Hear • Here Comes Santa Claus • I Saw Mommy Kissing Santa Claus • Let It Snow! Let It Snow! Let It Snow! • Merry Christmas, Darling • Silver Bells.
00311137 P/V/G $12.95

Vol. 13 Yuletide Favorites
Angels We Have Heard on High • Away in a Manger • Deck the Hall • The First Noel • Go, Tell It on the Mountain • Jingle Bells • Joy to the World • O Little Town of Bethlehem.
00311138 P/V/G $12.95

Vol. 14 Pop Ballads
Have I Told You Lately • I'll Be There for You • It's All Coming Back to Me Now • Looks Like We Made It • Rainy Days and Monday • Say You, Say Me • She's Got a Way • Your Song.
00311145 P/V/G $12.95

Vol. 15 Favorite Standards
Call Me • The Girl from Ipanema • Moon River • My Way • Satin Doll • Smoke Gets in Your Eyes • Strangers in the Night • The Way You Look Tonight.
00311146 P/V/G $12.95

Vol. 16 TV Classics
The Brady Bunch • Green Acres Theme • Happy Days • Johnny's Theme • Love Boat Theme • Mister Ed • The Munsters Theme • Where Everybody Knows Your Name.
00311147 P/V/G $12.95

Vol. 17 Movie Favorites
Back to the Future • Theme from E.T. • Footloose • For All We Know • Somewhere in Time • Somewhere Out There • Theme from Terms of Endearment • You Light Up My Life.
00311148 P/V/G $12.95

Vol. 18 Jazz Standards
All the Things You Are • Bluesette • Easy Living • I'll Remember April • Isn't It Romantic? • Stella by Starlight • Tangerine • Yesterdays.
00311149 P/V/G $12.95

Vol. 19 Contemporary Hits
Beautiful • Calling All Angels • Don't Know Why • If I Ain't Got You • 100 Years • This Love • A Thousand Miles • You Raise Me Up.
00311162 P/V/G $12.95

Vol. 20 R&B Ballads
After the Love Has Gone • All in Love Is Fair • Hello • I'll Be There • Let's Stay Together • Midnight Train to Georgia • Tell It like It Is • Three Times a Lady.
00311163 P/V/G $12.95

Vol. 21 Big Band
All or Nothing at All • Apple Honey • April in Paris • Cherokee • In the Mood • Opus One • Stardust • Stompin' at the Savoy.
00311164 P/V/G $12.95

Vol. 22 Rock Classics
Against All Odds • Bennie and the Jets • Come Sail Away • Do It Again • Free Bird • Jump • Wanted Dead or Alive • We Are the Champions.
00311165 P/V/G $12.95

Vol. 23 Worship Classics
Awesome God • How Majestic Is Your Name • Lord, Be Glorified • Lord, I Lift Your Name on High • Praise the Name of Jesus • Shine, Jesus, Shine • Step by Step • There Is a Redeemer.
00311166 P/V/G $12.95

Vol. 24 Les Misérables
Bring Him Home • Castle on a Cloud • Do You Hear the People Sing? • Drink with Me • Empty Chairs at Empty Tables • I Dreamed a Dream • A Little Fall of Rain • On My Own.
00311169 P/V/G $14.95

Vol. 25 The Sound of Music
Climb Ev'ry Mountain • Do-Re-Mi • Edelweiss • Maria • My Favorite Things • Sixteen Going on Seventeen • Something Good • The Sound of Music.
00311175 P/V/G $14.95

Vol. 26 Andrew Lloyd Webber Favorites
All I Ask of You • Amigos Para Siempre • As If We Never Said Goodbye • Everything's Alright • Memory • No Matter What • Tell Me on a Sunday • You Must Love Me.
00311178 P/V/G $12.95

Vol. 27 Andrew Lloyd Webber Greats
Any Dream Will Do • Don't Cry for Me Argentina • I Don't Know How to Love Him • The Music of the Night • The Phantom of the Opera • Unexpected Song • Whistle Down the Wind • With One Look.
00311179 P/V/G $12.95

Vol. 28 Lennon & McCartney
Eleanor Rigby • Hey Jude • The Long and Winding Road • Love Me Do • Lucy in the Sky with Diamonds • Nowhere Man • Strawberry Fields Forever • Yesterday.
00311180 P/V/G $12.95

Vol. 29 The Beach Boys
Barbara Ann • Be True to Your School • California Girls • Fun, Fun, Fun • Help Me Rhonda • I Get Around • Little Deuce Coupe • Wouldn't It Be Nice.
00311181 P/V/G $12.95

Vol. 30 Elton John
Candle in the Wind • Crocodile Rock • Daniel • Goodbye Yellow Brick Road • I Guess That's Why They Call It the Blues • Levon • Sorry Seems to Be the Hardest Word • Your Song.
00311182 P/V/G $12.95

Vol. 31 Carpenters
(They Long to Be) Close to You • For All We Know • I Won't Last a Day without You • Only Yesterday • Rainy Days and Mondays • Top of the World • We've Only Just Begun • Yesterday Once More.
00311183 P/V/G $12.95

Vol. 32 Bacharach & David
Alfie • Close to You • Do You Know the Way to San Jose • A House Is Not a Home • The Look of Love • Raindrops Keep Fallin' on My Head • What the World Needs Now Is Love • Wives and Lovers.
00311218 P/V/G $12.95

Vol. 33 Peanuts™
Blue Charlie Brown • Charlie Brown Theme • The Great Pumpkin Waltz • Joe Cool • Linus and Lucy • Oh, Good Grief • Red Baron • You're in Love, Charlie Brown.
00311227 P/V/G $12.95

Vol. 34 Charlie Brown Christmas
Christmas Is Coming • The Christmas Song • Christmas Time Is Here • Linus and Lucy • My Little Drum • O Tannenbaum • Skating • What Child Is This.
00311228 P/V/G $12.95

Vol. 35 Elvis Presley Hits
Blue Suede Shoes • Can't Help Falling in Love • Don't Be Cruel (To a Heart That's True) • Heartbreak Hotel • I Want You, I Need You, I Love You • It's Now or Never • Love Me • (Let Me Be Your) Teddy Bear.
00311230 P/V/G $12.95

Vol. 36 Elvis Presley Greats
All Shook Up • Don't • Jailhouse Rock • Love Me Tender • Loving You • Return to Sender • Too Much • Wooden Heart.
00311231 P/V/G $12.95

Vol. 37 Contemporary Christian
El Shaddai • Every Season • Here I Am • Jesus Will Still Be There • Let Us Pray • Place in This World • Who Am I • Wisdom.
00311232 P/V/G $12.95

Vol. 38 Duke Ellington – Standards
Caravan • Do Nothin' Till You Hear from Me • I Got It Bad and That Ain't Good • In a Sentimental Mood • It Don't Mean a Thing (If It Ain't Got That Swing) • Love You Madly • Mood Indigo • Sophisticated Lady.
00311233 P/V/G $14.95

Vol. 39 Duke Ellington – Classics
Come Sunday • Don't Get Around Much Anymore • I Let a Song Go out of My Heart • I'm Beginning to See the Light • In a Mellow Tone • Satin Doll • Solitude • Take the "A" Train.
00311234 P/V/G $14.95

Vol. 40 Showtunes
The Best of Times • Hello, Dolly! • I'll Know • Mame • Summer Nights • Till There Was You • Tomorrow • What I Did for Love.
00311237 P/V/G $12.95

Vol. 41 Rodgers & Hammerstein
Bali Ha'i • Do I Love You Because You're Beautiful? • Hello, Young Lovers • If I Loved You • It Might As Well Be Spring • Love, Look Away • Oh, What a Beautiful Mornin' • The Sweetest Sounds.
00311238 P/V/G $12.95

Vol. 42 Irving Berlin
Always • Blue Skies • Change Partners • Cheek to Cheek • Easter Parade • How Deep Is the Ocean (How High Is the Sky) • Puttin' on the Ritz • What'll I Do?
00311239 P/V/G $14.95

Vol. 43 Jerome Kern
Can't Help Lovin' Dat Man • A Fine Romance • The Folks Who Live on the Hill • I Won't Dance • I'm Old Fashioned • The Last Time I Saw Paris • Long Ago (And Far Away) • Ol' Man River.
00311240 P/V/G $14.95

Vol. 44 Frank Sinatra – Popular Hits
Come Fly with Me • Cycles • High Hopes • Love and Marriage • My Way • Strangers in the Night • (Love Is) The Tender Trap • Young at Heart.
00311277 P/V/G $14.95

Vol. 45 Frank Sinatra – Most Requested Songs
All the Way • The Birth of the Blues • From Here to Eternity • I've Got the World on a String • Theme from "New York, New York" • Night and Day • Time After Time • Witchcraft.
00311278 P/V/G $14.95

Vol. 46 Wicked
Dancing Through Life • Defying Gravity • For Good • I Couldn't Be Happier • I'm Not That Girl • Popular • What Is This Feeling? • The Wizard and I.
00311317 P/V/G $12.95

Vol. 47 Rent
I'll Cover You • Light My Candle • One Song Glory • Out Tonight • Rent • Seasons of Love • What You Own • Without You.
00311319 P/V/G $12.95

Vol. 48 Christmas Carols
God Rest Ye Merry, Gentlemen • Hark! The Herald Angels Sing • It Came upon the Midnight Clear • O Come, All Ye Faithful (Adeste Fideles) • O Holy Night • Silent Night • We Three Kings of Orient Are • What Child Is This?
00311332 P/V/G $12.95

Vol. 49 Holiday Hits
Frosty the Snow Man • Happy Xmas (War Is Over) • (There's No Place Like) Home for the Holidays • I'll Be Home for Christmas • Jingle-Bell Rock • Rockin' Around the Christmas Tree • Rudolph the Red-Nosed Reindeer • Santa Claus Is Comin' to Town.
00311333 P/V/G $12.95

FOR MORE INFORMATION, SEE YOUR LOCAL MUSIC DEALER, OR WRITE TO:

HAL•LEONARD CORPORATION
7777 W. BLUEMOUND RD. P.O. BOX 13819 MILWAUKEE, WI 53213

Visit Hal Leonard Online at www.halleonard.com

Prices, contents and availability subject to change without notice.

1206